Inquest

Books by Michael McGriff

Poetry

Inquest
Angel Sharpening its Beak
Eternal Sentences
Early Hour
Home Burial
Dismantling the Hills

Fiction

Our Secret Life in the Movies (with J.M. Tyree)

Translation

The Sorrow Gondola by Tomas Tranströmer

As Editor

To Build My Shadow a Fire:
The Poetry and Translations of David Wevill

Inquest

a poem

Michael McGriff

WHITE PINE PRESS / BUFFALO, NEW YORK

White Pine Press
P.O. Box 236
Buffalo, NY 14201
www.whitepine.org

Publication of this book was supported by public funds from the New York State Council on the Arts, with the support of Governor Kathy Hochul and the New York State Legislature, a State Agency.

Cover Image: Untitled photograph, Michael McGriff, 2022.

Printed and bound in the United States of America.

ISBN 978-1-945680-83-0

Library of Congress Control Number: 2024952452

Acknowledgments

The author thanks the editors of the following journals, where sections of this poem first appeared:

basalt: [When numbers]; [Why does the entirety of October]; [How often do the evergreens]; [Were you just humming]; [Was our first mistake]; [Was the final ingredient]; [Will this be the first winter]; [Ezra Pound, what was it like]; [Is the sand the last thing]; [Is the county dump the secret society]

NECK: [Why argue with the breakers]; [Rail spike, gas mask instructions—]; [Why isn't the color of ditchwater]; [When you delivered a pallet]; [How many evenings have ended]; [Where does the ocean hide]

New England Review: [Was that the sound of my brother]; [Shoveling this manure, why do I feel]; [Was that an owl or *Bicycle Thieves*]; [Does the common rat]

Poetry Northwest: [Is the river deep enough to swim?—even]; [Will it be trees or factories whose roots]; [When they exhumed Pablo Neruda]; [Is the lightning in Eastern Oregon]; [Is the blood moon stuffing ballots]; [Shouldn't my false starts]; [Does the rain list its grievances]; [Have the rhododendrons also stood]; [Can't you see the light on the bean field]; [Who dared the hermit crab to make]

Several sections of *Inquest* appear in the anthology *Bookstore Clerks & Significant Others* edited by Scott Landfield (Tsunami Press, 2023).

The epigraphs come from section LI of William O'Daly's translation of Pablo Neruda's *The Book of Questions* (Copper Canyon Press, 1991) and Charles Henri Ford's translation of Louis Aragon's "Treatise on Style" in Mary Ann Caws' anthology of surrealist writings, *The Milk Bowl of Feathers* (New Directions, 2018).

My sincere thanks to Emmy Newman, Zach Eddy, Court Fund, and Ryan Downum, who wrote down all their questions; to Sara Michas-Martin, Gerald Costanzo, Joseph Millar, and Dorianne Laux, who offered all their truths;

to Matthew Dickman, tireless advocate of this book; and to Gail Wronsky and Dennis Maloney, for answering a knock at the door.

Contents

Why did I return to the indifference
of the limitless ocean?

—Pablo Neruda

One wonders. No answer rises from the abyss.

—Louis Aragon

Was that the sound of my brother
getting arrested? Or was it

the moon collecting its debts
from the jimson weed? Perhaps

it was the surf throwing itself
into the jetty, failing to strike

a blue spark? Lovely ghost, is that you
at the end of the driveway trying

to convince the young deputy
that a set of brass knuckles

is only a paperweight, or have I fallen
asleep with the windows open,

overhearing the thorn apples
swap stories as the ocean shuffles

its eternal deck of black cards
in the last corner of summer?

✲

Was that my grandmother
restringing her fiddle,

or were those alder branches
scraping the downspout?

Do the moths hold grudges
against the wings of the moon?

*

If it's true that ghosts don't shit,
is it also true their jokes are terrible?

Was it real, when I heard
the trees comparing their debts?

Does the river wear gloves
when it dismantles a foot?

*

Why do I value the physics of a spark plug
more than the mouth of a scholar?

Is the fog on Blue Harbor jealous of gas and oil
mixed and burned into a trail of blue smoke?

Was that a wild turkey accosting an old woman,
or was that a man dancing with an ironing board?

*

Shoveling this manure, why do I feel
suddenly related to half the phone book?

How is the fresh paint on the black hinge
related to the crows stripping the tree

of its cherries? What is a parabola
if not the arrogance of symmetry,

and why do the cut halves of a sour apple
spin in opposite directions on the butcher's block?

✡

Have you already discovered the walls
are stuffed with straw and newspaper,

or are you still dancing to the radio
unplugged since 1941? Why is it today

that all women see their dead sons in me
the moment I slouch through a doorway?

Where did the hidden star keep its sack
of stripped bolts as it crept through the night?

☆

Why don't these canyons' painted hills
yell at me to hear their own voices?

Did the sheep in Sweden get so lost
they became the clouds my grandfather

tried to remember? If I keep scouring you
with kerosene, will I reveal the face of a deer?

*

How long is the equation between
the moon and this handful of rice?

Did I mention there are dead beetles
in my new pack of smokes, that the bones

in my hand have grown thin and blue
as the first snows in the Year of the Rabbit?

*

Was that an owl or *Bicycle Thieves*
projected onto the side of our barn?

Was that the back door or an old record
hissing beyond its final track?

Or was that the crunching of gravel
just past the end of the pavement?

✲

Does the common rat
support organized labor?

Is the smoke hidden inside a box knot
different than the smoke in a square knot?

Do you see my entire family driving to town
to watch my father buy Red Wing boots

with his first paycheck from the mill?
How many rivers will refuse to vote

in the primaries? Did the runoff
from the upstream chrome plant

turn the ferns orange as an eyelid
in the October moonlight?

*

Is the river deep enough to swim?—even
if it tucks a dark feather behind its ear?

Is it trespassing if you find a cloud
with its iron mouth pressed to the water?

How often is a dead man's eye fitted
to the milky head of a floating shad?

Is the hatch a winged shape shaped
by how we swim along the shore?

✡

Will it be trees or factories whose roots
grow down into my grave? What's it called

when a rope stretches two inches beyond
its limit? Will my final thoughts

reflect my pride over never using umbrellas,
or will I see a new mountain rise up from the sea?

Would I tire of crows if they finally wrote down
their opaque theories of the evening sky?

✲

When they exhumed Pablo Neruda
did they actually think he'd be there

holding the frayed end of a green rope?
Was his ribcage surrounding a pile

of brass keys? Do cormorants admire
the arithmetic of the zebra fish?

Why does all hair look the same
as the body sinks beneath the waves?

*

Is the lightning in Eastern Oregon
shaped like a question mark

before it leaves the womb? Is there
a finer thing than the back of a hand

as the body ages? Why not abandon
my ill-fitting jeans at the fire house?

Aren't you tired of that window
translating the light so literally?

Aren't I allowed to carry a passport
with the face of a mining burrow?

✲

Is the blood moon stuffing ballots
into the low firs? Is the final act

of the sparrow's atonement to return
the straw to the scarecrow's ribs?

As my brother steals the copper
from February's black spool,

is he perfectly situated between
heaven and earth? What is the space

between mirrors when they lie
pressed together?—does the light

unwind itself into the single image
of my mother painting on her eyebrows,

aligning her wig, one black degree
at a time, like a sextant,

with the dark burning points
and unborn-bright of the afterlife?

✲

Shouldn't my false starts
have a representative in Congress?

What if a brash lie is the only way
across this river? Am I more related

to Harry Truman or Genghis Khan?
Is my brother actually a boatyard

with a number instead of a name?
How many worms have written

memoirs featuring bait coolers
and careless children? Is it better

to let the moon work for us
or detain it at the border?

*

Does the rain list its grievances
in descending order? How old

are imaginary numbers? You don't
feel threatened by the heron's shadow

forming Xs across the millpond?
You don't have theories about

passing field sobriety tests?
Your uncle didn't advise you

to only hit a woman with an open fist?
When the sky is a thin slice of pink

across the gorge, why do the mountains
grow smaller the closer I get?

✲

Have the rhododendrons also stood
at the kitchen window, watching

a County Sheriff remove a child
from his parents? Do the angels

wax their cars each Friday night?
What's the midway point between blue

and green horses? Will I die without
seeing a coyote take down a caribou?

✲

Can't you see the light on the bean field
is a bloody gill? Does the gray jay know

we call it a whisky jack, that we rely on it
to lead us to the fresh carcass in the brush?

*

Who dared the hermit crab to make
a new home in the dead man's ear

and drag him across the sand
like the world's slowest comet?

☆

Why argue with the breakers
when a bloated pig and a car battery

are tossed ashore on the same
gray wave? Is that smudge

in the Milky Way one of God's
collapsed lungs? Why argue

aesthetics if you've never surrendered
to the October light of West Texas?

✲

Rail spike, gas mask instructions—
what brought you to gather dust

on my father's nightstand?
Is the surgeon's instrument tray

gleaming in the closet vying
for the attention of its friends,

or is it just admiring itself
in the button of an old suit?

✡

Why isn't the color of ditchwater
called Metal Fatigue? Is the Dog Star

ashamed of its endless boredom?
Why not build my house next to

the crematorium? How many heads
will eventually touch my mother's wigs?

Isn't blue snow equal to an owl
in the rain? If you've carried

a flashlight in a search party,
then why not be close to fire

when given the chance? Why
stop counting if it means

you can keep your eyes closed
long into the hours of the night?

*

When you delivered a pallet
of diapers to the women's shelter

did you notice the exquisite pen
on the edge of the receptionist's desk?

✡

How many evenings have ended
with a new couple arguing

over the definition of *parallax?*
Are those acetylene sparks

on the floor, or a spilled pile
of yellow toenail clippings?

Is that steam or smoke rising
from the field of bone-white cows?

Why have the years conspired
to bring my grandfather's hand tools

into my garage, and why
is it so exceptionally pleasing

to oil those instruments whose names
and functions I'll never learn?

*

Where does the ocean hide
when it loses faith? How many

oyster shells does it take to fill
my childhood? What if

the shore pines are only here
on loan, and that tangle of keys

on the warden's desk
is just a cruel trick of light?

*

Is it true the government is run
by a secret network of mushrooms?

Does the rain shed its tail
when trapped in a culvert?

How many times must the ocean
repeat itself? What if there's no

difference between sheet music
and a ransom note, and what if

our neighbor's metal roof ticking
in the sun makes the same noise

as my mother dropping one glass bead
after another into an empty beer can

on the first anniversary
of my brother's final disappearance?

✲

Why can't *Pneumatic* be the name
of a lost book in the Bible?

Shouldn't the ripples on the lake
move back toward the rock

the child threw after being told not to?
Don't the yellow birds in the cemetery

realize their smoke breaks ended
five minutes and ten ceremonial flags ago?

✲

How does the origin myth begin
that explains the stench of bears?

Would I be here to write this
had my father not enlisted

for Vietnam and gotten
stationed in Germany?

Why are these wooden crutches
and this bucket of pocket knives

the only things in the pawnshop
that don't fill me with despair?

✡

Do horses miss the days
when people ran wild

in alpine meadows?
Is that a strand

of the dying carpenter's hair
in the sparrow's nest?

As my father sits at the VFW
telling stories, is he drunk

or are those the acute
side effects of time travel?

✲

Brown rubber boa,
is it a merciless rumor,

or are you really the world's
most docile snake?

Is this charred log
our only real clue

about the afterlife?
Is the Russian novel

in my backpack
simply an appendix

for the margin notes
written in green ink

and lovely loops
on the very first page?

*

When the summit trail turns to tight
switchbacks, are you also thinking

of my friend who wrote *night is simply*
a shadow? Does the magpie sense

my shame in no longer remembering
what season became her final season,

or if her first name has two Ts or one?
What about the red dust and wildfire haze

allow the mind to black out one landscape
and replace it with another?

✲

In how many languages
is the ear of the rabbit

inside the year of the rabbit?
Is the gas cloud offended

when the mill owner tells
the mayor, *It's only steam?*

Did the rats ever get paid
for chiseling all those stars?

✲

When numbers
are finally abolished

how will you mark
your Jesus Year?

At what point in April
will a stranger's voice

come out of my mouth?
Did the migratory birds

land in my uncle's field
to attend a funeral?

If I'm just a minute late
for my own death

will it take months
to get it rescheduled?

*

Why does the entirety of October
feel like an old encyclopedia set?

Was television invented so the orca
could carry a dead calf on her back?

What's the crow have to do
with the breeze shooting up

from our stone well? Is it really called
a tyranny of crickets? Remember

when we were astronomers, huffing gas
until the stars burned in a field of ink?

✲

How often do the evergreens
change their outdated clothes?

Are they seriously forming
a committee to determine

which is worse, getting beaten
with a white extension cord

or an orange one? Can I exchange
these wings for the next size

even though I lost my receipt?
Can I make Richard Diebenkorn

an adverb so I can finally articulate
what I admire in all my friends

when they get drunk and start
rhyming with the half moon?

*

Were you just humming
the anthem for the apocalypse,

or was it the jingle for Shelby's
Gas-N-Go? How long

will it take this winter field
of burning tires to become

the dragon smoke
in a Chinese poem?

Do you really think
that drum of diesel

and loaded shotgun
is going to save you?

*

Was our first mistake
thinking we were better

than a floating bridge?
Is there a season where

I become a tidy metaphor
while my shadow becomes

twisted in its contradictions?
Do you have a permit

to touch the moon
as it screams across the bay?

✡

Was the final ingredient
a cold link of mooring chain?

Do wood smoke and fog
feel related in the same way

donkeys and anvils do?
Is the Oregon rain

all that's left of our oldest
memories of Atlantis?

✲

Will this be the first winter
the azaleas don't leak oil

from their crank cases? Is eternity
divided into different time zones?

Are you still in jail because I was
too drunk for jury duty? Remind me,

which side of the family is buried
between the river and the road?

☆

Ezra Pound, what was it like
to warm Li Po's feet against

your chest? Who was the first
to cross-thread the sky's drain plug?

Why do my curses feel watered down
when the trees shout them back at me?

Who died so I could buy
these wooden skis at a blind

woman's garage sale? Who will
take home this suit jacket whose

sleeves are lined with prime numbers,
wheel bearings, and flat gray skies?

✲

Is the sand the last thing
we have left to destroy?

Why can't I throw away
this box of ceramic fuses

or these commemorative
plates featuring minor

English royalty? Is this
the kind of storm

that uses the word *torpid*
in casual conversation?

Why not move to the
outskirts of color?

Cousin by marriage,
did your trick work—

keeping soup spoons
in the freezer to press

against the bruises
on your neck and face?

✡

Is the county dump the secret society
we've been warned about on AM radio?

Who among you ever tasted government
cheese? Did the Ferris Wheel originally spin

on its side? Was it a flywheel in a machine
the blue jays invented to mimic other machines?

☆

Was it a miracle, or something more sinister,
when I discovered I could stay underwater

forever? Did it feel inevitable the first time
you smelled the oil in Bakersfield?

Are you my killer, or just here to witness
the hundred-year bloom in the desert?

✡

Do the clock hands tremble more
as they age? Does the spiraling shell

feel dissatisfied with its form?
Are old women egg-shaped

because they get eaten in the afterlife?
Is the musical saw crying against it will?

✡

How often do our feet walk off
to beat their invisible wings

beneath the streetlights on the edge
of town? Will there be anything finer

than the fifty white goats I've hired
to rip the bluegrass from my grave?

✲

Does the rain ever dream
it's spent its whole life

in a ditch? At what point
did my father's hands

get sewn onto my wrists?
Is the ocean the only thing

that doesn't believe a list
has a final item? Does all this

water mean the sky's
doubling down on its bets?

*

Is the boomerang a pessimist
or an optimist? Is the light

at a parent's funeral attached
to an elaborate root system?

Do all shadows lose weight
in the steep light of winter?

Why not consider if the ostrich
grabbed the wrong set of wings

from his closet while the minister
carries on about ash and dust?

*

Are the foxgloves still rioting
along our gravel driveway?

Is that the sound of yellowjackets
drinking from a glass thread

in the dry creek bed, or is that
my grandmother's jaw clicking

through the night? Is that stand
of alders daring me to cross

their picket line? Who paid
the elk to forge my signature

in the muddy draw between
these two logging ridges?

✲

Can the way I feel about the stone jetty
go down on my permanent record?

Are the peacocks' voices still made
of charred floor joists and quicklime?

Will these waves of dead grass be governed
by the port authority or the ghosts of fish?

Are those boys in the stubble field
trying to reinstall a star in its socket,

or are those burning tires homegrown
traps for the low-hanging angels?

☆

Do the wildflowers trade in ideas?
Are acronyms forbidden in paradise?

Why not buy this starlight on credit?
Do the coffins enter a gallery

to choose among those of us who fall
within their meager budgets?

✲

Do my petty crimes fall under
the snow's jurisdiction?

Are they suspended in amber?
Is it still a felony if you know

where the key is, even if the hard
sky over the bay is already

unlocked? What if a rare snow
begins to fall? Brother, if two crows

share the same shadow, is it best
to lock all the windows, or should

we ready the five hundred
branches of the human heart?

✲

Among the dead, do the toothless
fight each other in parking lots?

Do they grow more suspicious
the farther they live from town?

If the day smells of hot rotors,
and if the paper wasps return

to nest in the soffits, and if angel
smoke gathers low in the fields,

will I be any closer to the horse's
cannon bone and the knife handle

it yearns to become? Isn't it the dead
who invent the sound of feather

over feather, and all the good light
just seconds beyond the visible world?

Michael McGriff is an author, editor, and translator whose work centers on the intersection of surrealism with place and poverty in rural America. He is the co-author, with J. M. Tyree, of the linked story collection *Our Secret Life in the Movies,* which was selected as one of NPR's Best Books of 2014. His poetry collections include *Inquest, Angel Sharpening its Beak, Eternal Sentences, Early Hour, Home Burial,* and *Dismantling the Hills.* He is the translator of Tomas Traströmer's *The Sorrow Gondola* and editor of a volume of David Wevill's essential writing, *To Build My Shadow a Fire.* From 2009-2014 he published and edited Tavern Books, a nonprofit literary press dedicated to poetry in translation and the revival of out-of-print contemporary classics. He is a former Stegner Fellow and Jones Lecturer at Stanford University, and his work has been honored with a Lannan Literary Fellowship, a *New York Times Book Review* "Editors' Choice," a Ruth Lilly Fellowship, and a grant from the National Endowment for the Arts. His writing has appeared in *The New York Times, FIELD, Kenyon Review, New England Review, Poetry, Bookforum, The Believer, Tin House, American Poetry Review, Poetry London,* and on NPR's Weekend Edition Sunday and PBS NewsHour. He has taught creative writing at Stanford University, The Michener Center for Writers, and Lewis & Clark College, and for several years has mentored young writers as a Visiting Writer at American International School in Vienna, Austria, and as a faculty member in the *Kenyon Review* Young Writers Workshop. He serves as co-director of the creative writing program at the University of Idaho.

THE WHITE PINE PRESS POETRY PRIZE

Vol. 30: *Inquest* by Michael McGriff. Selected by Gail Wronsky.

Vol. 29: *Easy Victims to the Charitable Deceptions of Nostalgia* by Emily Schulten. Selected by Marc Vincenz.

Vol. 28: *A Tree Becomes a Room* by J. P. White.
Selected by Danusha Laméris.

Vol. 27: *Blue If Only I Could Tell You* by Richard Tillinghast.
Selected by Joe Wilkins.

Vol. 26: *The Book of Mirrors* by Yun Wang.
Selected by Jennifer Kwon Dobbs.

Vol. 25: *Aflame* by Gary McDowell.
Selected by Sean Thomas Dougherty.

Vol. 24: *Our Age of Anxiety* by Henry Israeli.
Selected by Kathleen McGookey.

Vol. 23: *Secure Your Own Mask* by Shaindel Beers.
Selected by Alan Michael Parker.

Vol. 22: *Bread From a Stranger's Oven* by Janlori Goldman.
Selected by Laure-Anne Bosselaar.

Vol. 21: *The Brighter House* by Kim Garcia.
Selected by Jericho Brown.

Vol. 20: *Some Girls* by Janet McNally.
Selected by Ellen Bass.

Vol. 19: *Risk* by Tim Skeen.
Selected by Gary Young.

Vol. 18: *What Euclid's Third Axiom Neglects to Mention About Circles* by Carolyn Moore. Selected by Patricia Spears Jones.

Vol. 17: *Notes from the Journey Westward* by Joe Wilkins. Selected by Samuel Green.

Vol. 16: *Still Life* by Alexander Long. Selected by Aliki Barnstone.

Vol. 15: *Letters From the Emily Dickinson Room* by Kelli Russell Agodon. Selected by Carl Dennis.

Vol. 14: *In Advance of All Parting* by Ansie Baird. Selected by Roo Borson.

Vol. 13: *Ghost Alphabet* by Al Maginnes. Selected by Peter Johnson.

Vol. 12: *Paper Pavilion* by Jennifer Kwon Dobbs. Selected by Genie Zeiger.

Vol. 11: *The Trouble with a Short Horse in Montana* by Roy Bentley. Selected by John Brandi.

Vol. 10: *The Precarious Rhetoric of Angels* by George Looney. Selected by Nin Andrews.

Vol. 9: *The Burning Point* by Frances Richey. Selected by Stephen Corey.

Vol. 8: *Watching Cartoons Before Attending A Funeral* by John Surowiecki. Selected by C.D. Wright.

Vol. 7: *My Father Sings, To My Embarrassment* by Sandra Castillo. Selected by Cornelius Eady.

Vol. 6: *If Not For These Wrinkles of Darkness* by Stephen Frech. Selected by Pattiann Rogers.

Vol. 5: *Trouble in History* by David Keller.
Selected by Pablo Medina.

Vol. 4: *Winged Insects* by Joel Long.
Selected by Jane Hirshfield.

Vol. 3: *A Gathering of Mother Tongues* by Jacqueline Joan Johnson.
Selected by Maurice Kenny.

Vol. 2: *Bodily Course* by Deborah Gorlin.
Selected by Mekeel McBride.

Vol. 1: *Zoo & Cathedral* by Nancy Johnson.
Selected by David St. John.